SNAKES

DIAMONDBACK RATTLESNAKES

James E. Gerholdt
ABDO & Daughters

Published by Abdo & Daughters, 4940 Viking Drive, Suite 622, Edina, Minnesota 55435.

Library bound edition distributed by Rockbottom Books, Pentagon Tower, P.O. Box 36036, Minneapolis, Minnesota 55435.

Printed in the United States.

Cover Photo credit: James Gerholdt
Interior Photo credits: Peter Arnold, Inc. pages 7, 9, 11, 13, 15, 17, 19, 21

James Gerholdt, page 5

Edited by Julie Berg

Library of Congress Cataloging-in-Publication Data

Gerholdt, James E., 1943
    Diamondback rattlesnake / James E. Gerholdt.
        p. cm. — (Snakes)
Includes bibliographical references (p. 23) and index.
Summary: Provides a wealth of basic information about this poisonous pit viper, including its physical characteristics, habitat. Food habits and defense mechanisms.
ISBN 1-56239-515-7
1. Western diamondback rattlesnake—Juvenile literature. [1. Western diamondback rattlesnake. 2. Poisonous snakes. 3. Snakes.] I. Title. II. Series: Gerholdt, James E., 1943- Snakes.
QL666.069G473   1995
597.96—dc20   95-9048
                                                                                    CIP
                                                                                    AC

About the Author

Jim Gerholdt has been studying reptiles and amphibians for more than 40 years. He has presented lectures and displays throughout the state of Minnesota for 9 years. He is a founding member of the Minnesota Herpetological Society and is active in conservation issues involving reptiles and amphibians in India and Aruba, as well as Minnesota.

Contents

DIAMONDBACK RATTLESNAKES

Rattlesnakes belong to one of the 11 families of snakes. Snakes are **reptiles**, which are **vertebrates**. This means they have a backbone, just like a human.

Rattlesnakes are **cold blooded**. They get their body temperature from lying in the sun, on a warm rock, or the warm ground. If they are too cool, their bodies won't work. If they get too hot, they will die. The rattlesnake gets its name from the rattle on the end of its tail.

The western diamondback rattlesnake.

SIZES

The western diamondback is the second-largest rattlesnake. Only the eastern diamondback rattlesnake is larger.

The length of a rattlesnake is measured from the tip of the nose to the base of the rattle. The largest western diamondback rattlesnake ever recorded was just under seven feet (2 m) in length. The largest eastern diamondbacks are eight feet (2.4 m). It is difficult and dangerous to measure snakes this long.

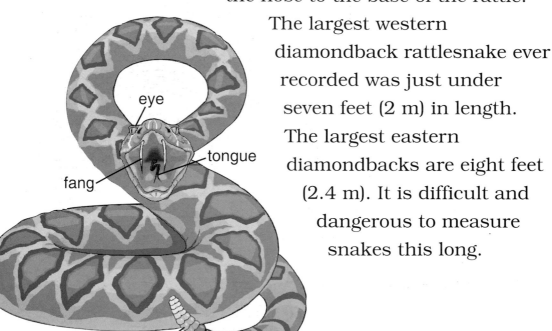

eye

tongue

fang

rattle

These are western diamondbacks, the second-largest rattlesnake.

The average size of western diamondbacks is three to four feet (.9 to 1.2 m) in length. The eastern diamondback is 3.5 to 5.5 feet (1 to 1.7 m) long.

COLORS

Western diamondback rattlesnakes are usually a dusty-looking gray to brown color. Some are much prettier, and may be reddish to pinkish gray. Some from New Mexico are very dark. A few are yellow with pink eyes. These are called **albinos**.

On this snake's back is a row of diamond shapes, from where this rattler gets its name. These diamonds are a dark gray brown to brown in color.

The eastern diamondback has whitish stripes on the side of its head. Its body is olive green to dark brown. On the back is a row of darker diamond shapes. Each shape has a lighter center and a yellow edge.

The diamondback's tail has black rings on a whitish background. It looks like a raccoon's tail. The base of the rattle is black. Another name for the diamondback is the coon-tailed rattler, because of its ringed tail.

The diamondback rattlesnake has white and black stripes on its tail.

WHERE THEY LIVE

Diamondback rattlesnakes live in many different **habitats**. They are found on flat, open plains, rocky hillsides, and canyons. They live in cactus, **sagebrush**, and grasslands. They are most common in dry lowlands. But they may also be found in the mountains as high as 5,000 feet (1,524 m).

Diamondbacks often use old **rodent burrows** for shelter. Sometimes they hide under boards and pieces of cardboard or tin. But no matter where they may live, diamondbacks blend in with their surroundings. This is called **camouflage**.

Diamondback rattlesnakes are found in many different habitats.

WHERE THEY ARE FOUND

Diamondback rattlesnakes are found in North America. In the United States, the eastern diamondback is found along the southern and eastern coasts from Louisiana (LA) through Florida to North Carolina (NC).

The western diamondback is found from Arkansas (AR) to southeastern California southward through most of Texas into Mexico and Baja California. Several Gulf of California islands also have diamondbacks.

A western diamondback den site in the North Texas badlands.

SENSES

Rattlesnakes and humans share four of the same senses. They have trouble seeing anything that isn't moving. Their **pupils** are **vertical** to help them to see in the dark, where much of their activity takes place. These vertical pupils open up in the dark to let in more light.

Rattlesnakes don't have ears, and cannot hear. But they can feel **vibrations** through bones in the lower jaw.

Smell is the snake's most important sense. It uses its tongue with which to smell. Rattlesnakes also have two heat-sensing pits between the mouth and nostrils. This is why they are also called pit vipers.

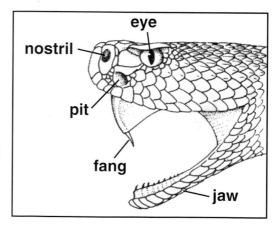

14

The diamondback rattlesnake smells with its tongue. It has heat-sensing pits between the mouth and nostrils.

DEFENSE

Camouflage is the diamondback's most important defense against enemies. If an enemy can't see it, the rattlesnake is safe. But if an enemy does find it, or is about to step on it, the rattlesnake uses its second-most important defense. It rattles!

The rattle's noise comes from the loose pieces of the rattle that rub against each other when the snake shakes its tail. If rattling doesn't work, the snake may strike and bite.

The fangs are long and can **inject venom** into the enemy. If enough venom is injected, the enemy—including people—may die!

The rattle's noise comes from loose pieces of the rattle that rub against each other when the snake shakes its tail.

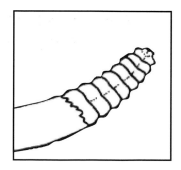

*A diamondback rattlesnake will rattle its
tail to scare off its enemies.*

FOOD

    Diamondback rattlesnakes eat other animals. They may also eat eggs if they can find them. Snakes do not eat fruit or vegetables.

    A small rattlesnake will eat small **rodents** and lizards. A larger snake will eat rats or even rabbits. The diamondback will keep still and wait for an animal to come by. It will use its tongue, heat-sensing pits, and the bones in the lower jaw to sense its **prey**.

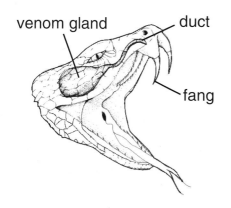

venom gland   duct

fang

Venom is made in the venom glands. The glands are on both sides of the snake's head and lie outside the main jaw muscles toward the back of the head. When the snake bites, the venom travels from each gland through the ducts and the hollow fangs, and into the prey.

*A common kingsnake eating a
diamondback rattlesnake.*

When the animal is close enough, the snake will strike and **inject** the **venom**. The prey won't go very far before it dies. The rattlesnake will follow it with its tongue and then swallow it whole!

BABIES

Like all of the rattlesnakes, diamondbacks give birth to live young. The female will have eight to fourteen babies. The babies are nine to fourteen inches (23 to 36 cm) in length. The size and number of the young depends on the size of the female.

The babies are born with the beginning of the rattle on their tail. After seven to ten days, the skin is shed for the first time. Only the rattle remains until it breaks off.

After this first shed, a new piece of rattle is added each time the skin is shed. This may happen several times in one year. So, you cannot tell the age of a rattlesnake by the number of its rattles!

You can't tell how old a diamondback rattlesnake is by the number of rattles it has on its tail.

GLOSSARY

Albino (al-BYE-no) - An animal with pink eyes and very light skin.

Burrow - A hole dug in the ground by an animal for shelter or protection.

Camouflage (CAM-a-flaj) - The skill to blend in with the surroundings.

Cold-blooded - Receiving body temperature from an outside source.

Habitat (HAB-uh-tat) - An area in which an animal lives.

Inject - To force liquid into the body through a hollow needle or fangs.

Prey - An animal that is eaten by other animals for food.

Pupil - The dark center of the eye.

Reptile (REP-tile) - A scaly-skinned animal with a backbone.

Rodent (ROW-dent) - An animal with large front teeth, that are used for gnawing. Rats, mice, and squirrels are rodents.

Sagebrush (SAYJ-brush) - A grayish-green, bushy plant, common on the dry plains of western North America.

Species (SPEE-seas) - A kind or type.
Venom (VEN-um) - Poison that is used to kill animals for food.
Vertebrate (VER-tuh-brit) - An animal with a backbone.
Vertical (VER-tih-kull) - Up and down.
Vibration - (vie-BRAY-shun) A quivering or trembling motion.

BIBLIOGRAPHY

Conant, Roger and Joseph T. Collins. *A Field Guide to Reptiles and Amphibians of Eastern and Central North America* - Third Edition. Houghton Mifflin Company, 1991.

Ernst, Carl H. and Roger W. Barbour. *Snakes of Eastern North America.* George Mason University Press, 1989.

Tennant, Alan. *A Field Guide to the Snakes of Texas.* Texas Monthly Press, *1985.*
—————.*The Snakes of Texas.* Texas Monthly Press, 1984.

Index